pocket posh®

Coloring
BOOK

· · · · · · · · · · · · · · · · ·

VINTAGE DESIGNS
FOR FUN & RELAXATION

· · · · · · · · · · · · · · · · ·

Andrews McMeel
Publishing®

Kansas City · Sydney · London

POCKET POSH® COLORING BOOK
VINTAGE DESIGNS FOR FUN & RELAXATION

Andrews McMeel Publishing, LLC
an Andrews McMeel Universal company
1130 Walnut Street, Kansas City, Missouri 64106

www.andrewsmcmeel.com

15 16 17 18 19 SHZ 10 9 8 7 6 5 4 3

ISBN: 978-1-4494-5873-7

www.shutterstock.com
With thanks to Hannah Davies for her original artworks

ATTENTION: SCHOOLS AND BUSINESSES
Andrews McMeel books are available at quantity
discounts with bulk purchase for educational, business, or
sales promotional use. For information, please e-mail the
Andrews McMeel Publishing Special Sales Department:
specialsales@amuniversal.com.

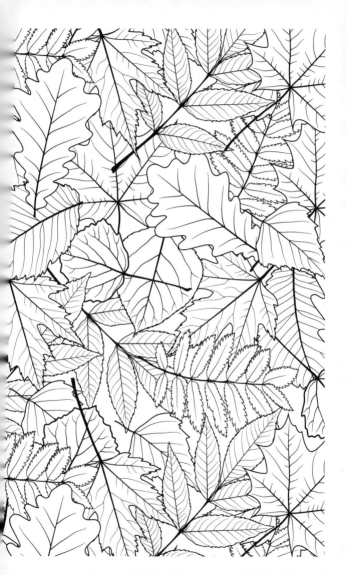

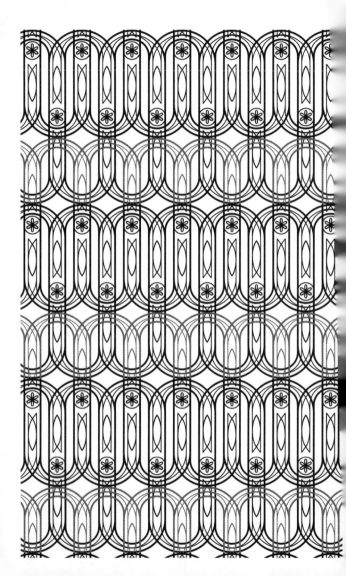

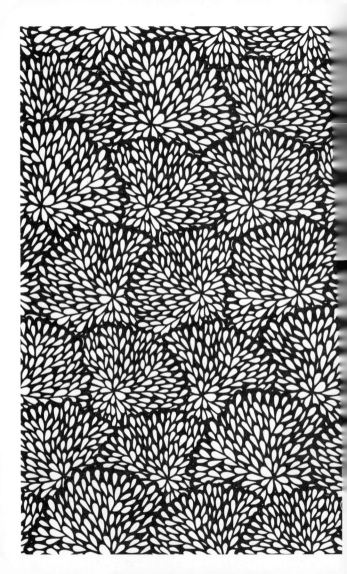